# The Rape of Nanking: The History and Legacy during the Second Sino-Japanese War

### By Charles River Editors

**A Picture of Victims**

## About Charles River Editors

**Charles River Editors** provides superior editing and original writing services across the digital publishing industry, with the expertise to create digital content for publishers across a vast range of subject matter. In addition to providing original digital content for third party publishers, we also republish civilization's greatest literary works, bringing them to new generations of readers via ebooks.

Sign up here to receive updates about free books as we publish them, and visit Our Kindle Author Page to browse today's free promotions and our most recently published Kindle titles.

# Introduction

## The Rape of Nanking

"From a military point of view, the taking of Nanking may be considered a victory for the Japanese army but judging it from the moral law, it is a defeat and a national disgrace—which will hinder cooperation and friendship with China for years to come, and forever lose her the respect of those living in Nanking today." - Minnie Vautrin, missionary, writing in her diary during the Nanking Massacre (Hu, 2010, 41).

"When you're talking about the Japanese military, thievery and rape just come with the territory. We stabbed them with bayonets, cut open pregnant women and took out the child. I killed five or six of them myself. I used to do some pretty brutal things." - Kodaira Yoshio, former Japanese soldier (Honda, 2015, 122).

"This is the shortest day of the year, but it still contains twenty-four hours of this hell on earth." - Dr. Robert Wilson, diary entry in Nanking, December 21st, 1937 (Brook, 1999, 219).

Three days of plundering traditionally befell cities taken by storm, a fate usually avoided by those surrendering before the first attacking soldier penetrated beyond the outer walls. In Europe and areas influenced by Enlightenment thinkers, this practice faded rapidly after the Napoleonic Wars. In 1937, however, as the Imperial Army of Japan invaded China, this custom returned in a horrifying new form – the Rape of Nanking or the Nanking Massacre, a bloodbath lasting more than six weeks and possibly claiming more than a quarter of a million lives.

Even the Japanese participating in the Nanking Massacre provided no rationale for their actions. They made no effort to explain it as a measure to terrorize other Chinese cities into surrender, or even to extract the location of hidden valuables. Instead, the Rape appears on the page of history as a psychopathic orgy of sadism for sadism's sake. Insatiably driven by hatred and, apparently, an unabashed relish for cruelty, the Japanese soldiery abandoned any semblance of restraint.

Women of every age, from small children to ancient elders, suffered innumerable rapes, in many cases dying from the mass raping alone. Those who did not die from sexual assault suffered death in other forms – shot, decapitated, or tortured to death once the soldiers found themselves sexually exhausted. Other women suffered fatal sexual torture involving the introduction of sharp foreign objects into their vagina or the placement of firecrackers or live grenades inside. At least one soldier, Kodaira Yoshio, so enjoyed torturing women to death that he returned to Japan as a serial killer, treating his Japanese victims in the same fashion as Chinese women until caught and executed.

The Japanese hacked men to death, shot them, used them for live bayonet practice, drowned them, locked them in sheds and burned them, or buried them alive. Even farm animals suffered mutilation, shooting, or burning while locked in their barns. Unburied corpses lay in heaps everywhere, while the Japanese continued to harry and slaughter the survivors for week after week. A choking stench hung over the city in the summer heat.

A number of foreign people on the scene attempted to save some of the Chinese from the massacre and, in some cases, succeeded. Their neutral status gave them the ability to move around Nanking without – in most cases – suffering assault or murder by the swarms of Japanese troops glutting themselves endlessly on human pain and death. They also photographed the nearly inconceivable images of bloodshed, creating a stark, permanent record of one of World

War II's leading atrocities.

Even Third Reich personnel in the city interceded in a sometimes futile effort to rescue victims from their tormentors. At the end of the city's long harrowing, the world knew clearly, if it did not before, that the Japanese of Tojo and Hirohito showed a very different spirit than the exquisitely genteel and chivalric men of the Russo-Japanese War of 1905. The fight against Imperial Japan represented not merely an effort to avoid being conquered, but for survival itself.

*The Rape of Nanking: The History and Legacy of the Notorious Massacre during the Second Sino-Japanese War* chronicles one of the most infamous events of the 20th century. Along with pictures of important people, places, and events, you will learn about the rape of Nanking like never before, in no time at all.

The Rape of Nanking: The History and Legacy of the Notorious Massacre during the Second Sino-Japanese War

About Charles River Editors

Introduction

Japanese imperialism on the Asian mainland began long before the usually recognized start of World War II. Following Admiral Perry's expedition to open the xenophobic Tokugawa Shogunate to foreign trade in 1852, the Japanese rapidly adopted new technologies and used them to impose their will on the neighboring Asian mainland. For the second time in history, Japan exerted its dominance over Korea, then clashed with China in 1894 over the Korean question. The Japanese decisively defeated the backward and moribund Chinese imperial navy and imposed a victor's treaty.

**Tokugawa Clan Crest**

The Japanese next directed their aggression, successfully, against the Russians in the 1905 Russo-Japanese war. Though the Japanese observed the rules of "civilized warfare" punctiliously during the conflict, the fierce, utterly mercilessly warrior culture of the samurai lurked just beneath the surface, waiting to emerge in the coming decades.

The doom of Nanking emerged from the collision between seemingly endless civil war that swept China from 1911 until well after the end of World War II, killing approximately 20 million people, and Japanese imperial ambitions in Manchuria in the 1930s. The Japanese had all the hallmarks of a major maritime power, similar to Great Britain or the United States of America, yet decided to develop their land forces and fight large-scale land wars, discarding the advantages of a focus on oceanic strategy.

Seeking economic independence and the resources needed to continue their modernization as a twentieth century military power, the Japanese manufactured a transparent pretext in 1931 and attacked northern China, exploiting the ongoing bloodbath between the Chinese Nationalists and Communists:

> "On 18 September 1931 Japan launched a full-scale invasion of Manchuria in response to an explosion near Shenyang, bending a few meters of its railway track, which it repaired by 6 a.m. the following day. [...] Although the Japanese government accused the Chinese of perpetrating the vandalism, before long its own internal investigation held members of the Japanese army responsible." (Paine, 2012, 13).

The Japanese characterized this massive onslaught as an "Incident," for a very simple reason. Many of Japan's supplies came from the United States, as did those of the Chinese. The U.S. Neutrality Act forbade selling anything to countries engaged in aggressive war. The Japanese used the term "incident" as a legalistic euphemism for their war, thus enabling them to continue trading with U.S. businesses, at least temporarily.

Manchuria represented a rich prize for the hungrily expansionist Japanese, supplying China with most of its oil, gold, and iron, and accounting for around a third of the entire nation's economic activity. This undefended economic powerhouse quickly fell to the Japanese "Kanto Army," which, bizarrely, set up "Henri Puyi," the deposed Chinese emperor, as the emperor of the new puppet state of Manchukuo.

The Japanese civil government attempted to reign in the ascendant military, but met with assassinations and broader expulsion of several cabinets in response. The Japanese attacked Shanghai, the center of foreign investment, in 1932, in an effort to coerce the Chinese into accepting the "independence" of Manchukuo, or "Land of the Manchus." The Imperial government offered, in effect, to trade Shanghai back to the Chinese in exchange for official recognition of their puppet state. This scheme backfired, enraging the Chinese and briefly uniting many of them behind the Nationalist leader Chiang Kai-Shek.

The Japanese developed Manchuria economically, transforming it into a relatively modern industrial powerhouse filled with mines and factories. Manchuria furnished the dynamo permitting the Japanese war machine to continue functioning.

The Manchurians themselves earned approximately 150% of the money received by the highest-paid industrial workers elsewhere in China, yet this did not translate into a higher standard of living. The Japanese siphoned off almost all production for their own uses, leading to a profound lack of consumer goods and a local economy providing only basic necessities. The Japanese economy, meanwhile, boomed, recovering swiftly from the worldwide Great Depression of the 1930s, a disaster caused by the survival of the antiquated gold standard in an era of economic transformation.

The Japanese, however, continued their aggression, steadily seizing additional provinces to add to their prize. They left the League of Nations in 1933 in response to that body's condemnation of their actions. In part, their demographic explosion provided the impetus to expansionism, with a population that rose from 30 million to 65 million in the course of just a few generations. Hashimoto Kingoro, a Lieutenant Colonel, wrote:

"There are only three ways left to Japan to escape from the pressures of surplus population... emigration, advance into world markets, and expansion of territory.  The first door, emigration, has been barred to us by the anti-Japanese immigration     policies of other countries. The second door... is being pushed shut by tariff barriers    and the abrogation of commercial treaties. What should Japan do when two of the         three doors have been closed against her?" (Chang, 1997, 26-27).

Of course, the Japanese made conditions much more difficult for themselves due to their naked brutality, which appalled even the most profit-minded foreign business owners, and their inability to stop. Had they consolidated their gains in Manchukuo and worked to build its economic strength alongside that of Japan, their involvement in later warfare, including the catastrophic defeat in World War II, might well have been avoided.

During the mid-1930s, Chiang Kai-Shek believed the Japanese too strong and too entrenched in Manchuria to oust with the forces available to China. Instead, he concentrated on his war against the communists, using a gradual strategy in which an army of 800,000 men moved forward into communist territory, constructing a network of blockhouses as they went to control the countryside. Chiang Kai-Shek signed the Tanggu Truce with the Japanese in mid-1933 to buy himself time, causing them to withdraw north of the Great Wall of China.

**Chiang Kai-Shek**

The Tanggu Truce proved nearly worthless and the Japanese seized not only Mongolia, but also resumed advances south of the Great Wall as soon as they created pretexts that seemed adequate to them. The Japanese turned Mongolia into "Mengkukuo," under a puppet ruler descended from Genghis Khan himself and bearing a name that would not be out of place in "Gulliver's Travels" – Demchugdongrub.

## Chapter 2: The Second Sino-Japanese War in 1937

Chiang Kai-Shek, later scorned due to associations with fascist leaders he, in fact, largely despised, led his Nationalists in a highly successful series of reforms in 1935, 1936, and early 1937. The Nationalists jettisoned the destructive silver standard, with its extreme volatility (second only to the gold standard for economic harmfulness), and instituted a widespread program of rural credit to rescue farmers from the effects of the long civil war.

Tax reforms eliminated unnecessary burdens and the Chinese economy expanded vigorously. A full recovery did not occur, but it never had a chance to – no economic program could fully restore a huge, complex country battered by 25 years of civil war in just two years, and later criticisms appear objectively unfair to the Nationalists.

De facto, the Second Sino-Japanese War began in 1931 when the Japanese invaded and occupied Manchuria and created their puppet state of Manchukuo. However, 1937 still represents a change in the pattern of conflict as the piecemeal advance of the Japanese army grew into a juggernaut-like onrush that disregarded all previous agreements with Chiang Kai-Shek. Chiang's policy of dealing with the crippling internal struggle first, then with the Japanese once China unified, foundered on the rock of events outside his control.

The fatal breach occurred on the night of July 7th, 1937, a confluence of three "7s" particularly ominous in Chinese numerology. The night, hot and brilliantly illuminated by a full moon, prompted a Japanese unit stationed near the Yongding River's Marco Polo Bridge to carry out night exercises. During the maneuvers, one Japanese soldier went missing, and portions of his unit crossed the Marco Polo Bridge to the Chinese side, ostensibly to look for him.

The soldier soon appeared, unharmed, but the Chinese soldiers from the 29th Army saw Japanese riflemen on their side of the river and opened fire. A short firefight ensued that ended with the Japanese retreating. The Japanese company commander called his Chinese counterpart by telephone and apologized, and the Chinese officer responded in a similar manner, both men seeking avoidance of another "incident."

The Japanese officer's immediate superior, however – the man in charge of the brigade – had less pacific intentions. He ordered the artillery at his disposal to bombard the Chinese headquarters and barracks on the other side of the Yongding River. As shells plowed through walls and tore apart men's bodies with blasts of shrapnel, the Chinese commander, goaded past any caution, ordered the batteries available to him to return fire, resulting in a vicious artillery duel.

**Yongding River, under the Marco Polo Bridge. Photo by Fanghong.**

The Japanese responded by moving hundreds of thousands of soldiers to attack southward and confront the "atrocious" Chinese army. The communist Mao Zedong publicly pretended to offer support to Chiang Kai-Shek and the Nationalists, but secretly plotted treachery, intending to leave the Nationalists and Japanese to maul each other so that his Red Army could pick up the pieces:

> "On July 31, however, showing his intention to avoid serious combat with the Japanese, Mao radioed his military lieutenants that the previous order was for propaganda purposes. In reality, he said, the troops should move slowly. In particular, they could 'move 50 li [500 meters] each day, and pause one day after every three days.'" (Taylor, 2009, 147).

**Mao Zedong**

The Japanese invaded Hebei Province first. Soon, China and Korea hosted no less than 21 Japanese divisions. The Chinese fought back, and, though the Japanese ultimately overwhelmed them and drove them back, the victory came at a high price. Around 100,000 Japanese soldiers suffered injury or death by the end of 1937, with the war destined to continue even more viciously for years, lasting into the 1940s.

Chiang Kai-Shek attempted to halt the Japanese at Shanghai, both for reasons of national prestige and in the hope of drawing the western powers into the struggle on his side. Thousands of foreigners lived in the rich trading port and immense business interests from Europe and the United States maintained important branches there. The Shanghai campaign began on August 11th, when the Nationalist air force attempted to bomb the Japanese warships in Shanghai harbor but instead, incompetently, struck the city's main foreign quarter, killing more than 1,300 foreign civilians.

The Nationalists mustered more than half a million military personnel (including air crews and support units) during their counterattack on Shanghai. Street fighting began on August 13th and initially the Chinese forced the Japanese marines back to a precarious foothold on the city wharves. However, the Japanese soon put 75,000 more men ashore. In brutal fighting in the streets and along the Whangpoo riverbank, the Japanese pushed the Chinese steadily back, albeit while sustaining thousands of wounded and dead.

At this pivotal juncture, even Zhou Enlai urged Mao to commit the communist Chinese Red Army forces to the struggle, fighting alongside their Nationalist counterparts against the common enemy of their nation. Coldly, Mao refused, preferring to see hundreds of thousands of Chinese die and extensive new territories fall under Japanese control if this raised the odds of his eventually defeating Chiang Kai-Shek. Mao called this the "Defeat for All" strategy.

On November 5th, 1937, the Japanese played their trump card. Intelligence reports indicated Chiang Kai-Shek – to his later open regret – withdrew the men guarding Hangzhou Bay on Shanghai's southern flank. One hundred warships from the Imperial Japanese Navy (IJN) 4th Fleet put three divisions, the 6th Kumamoto Division, the 114th Utsunomiya Division, and the 18th Kurume Division, ashore in Hangzhou Bay.

This force, known as the Japanese 10th Army, drove northward, trying to cut off Chiang Kai-Shek's men in a salient bounded by their lines to the west, the Yangtze River to the north, and the other Japanese forces (and the ocean) to the east and south. The Japanese used balloon-based propaganda to exaggerate the numbers of this force and terrorize the men risking being trapped in Shanghai, as a Japanese newspaper reported:

> "At noon on the 6th, a large advertising balloon unfolded and floated high in the skies over the north bank of the Suzhou River, and at the same time a great war cry suddenly arose from our troops. Look! Can you not clearly read what is written on the balloon floating lazily in the low rain clouds south of the Yangtze River? 'One million Japanese troops land north of Hangzhou Bay.'" (Honda, 2015, 9).

Regardless of the overblown figure of one million Japanese soldiers (which would require 10,000 men squeezed onto each warship, besides being more than Japan had under arms in 1937), deadly peril threatened the Nationalist Chinese soldiers. A very real possibility of encirclement loomed, after which massacre would inevitably ensue. Chiang Kai-Shek ordered a retreat on November 8th, but not before his corps of 30,000 young officers sustained 70% casualties and his army suffered 187,000 soldiers WIA or KIA.

## Chapter 3: The Battle of Nanking

Having ejected the Chinese from Shanghai at a cost of 9,115 deaths and 31,257 WIA, the Japanese pressed their advantage by following the fleeing Nationalist forces towards their capital of Nanking. The Japanese military also fanned out to snap up a number of key provincial capitals while the Chinese remained off balance following their defeat.

A German named Horst Baerensprung left a vivid account of the retreating Nationalists marching through the winter rain:

> "From a suburb of Nanking, I watched for almost seven hours as troops passed along the rutted muddy road. […] Even most of the officers were on foot […] The rain whipped at them mercilessly, incessantly […] The clouds hung so low that you could almost grab hold of them. The Purple Mountain and Lion Hill, the hallmarks of Nanking, were lost in fog. […] I looked at these carefully wrapped machine guns and then at those soldiers, who were soaked to the bone […] Christ was probably thinking of times like these when he advised his disciples: 'He that hath no sword, let him sell his garment and buy one.'" (Rabe, 1998, 24).

The Battle of Nanking began on December 1st, 1937. Chiang Kai-Shek, in his embattled capital, took overall command of the forces remaining at his disposal. In desperation, Chiang appealed to the Russian dictator Josef Stalin for Soviet troops to aid in throwing back the Japanese. Stalin responded that if he entered the conflict, the western powers might view him as victimizing Japan and enter the war against him. However, he did continue to send tanks, aircraft, and other military vehicles to the Nationalists, offering the support to the front-line Chinese that his fellow communist Mao denied.

Defending the sturdy walls of the city, and manning a series of pillboxes with interlocking fields of fire, the Chinese fought for days with dogged courage. The crack 88th Division died almost to a man, along with its senior officers, but took 566 Japanese KIA with them and wounded more than 1,500 additional soldiers. The Japanese, however, possessed superior weapons, plus better training than most (though not all) of the Chinese divisions. Using heavy artillery, the Japanese slowly battered the defenses to pieces, leveling part of the city and setting other portions ablaze.

Chiang Kai-Shek and his wife left the city by air on December 7th, while the reformed warlord Tang Shengzhi remained willingly to fight a rearguard action. Finally, on December 12th, the suicidal courage of Japanese soldiers with bamboo ladders enabled them to take the Zhonghua Gate in Nanking's walls. At the same time, a unit of tanks crashed through the Shuixi Gate and burst into the city.

**Tang Shengzhi**

Tang Shengzhi ordered the remaining soldiers to break out. Thousands died, drowning in the Yangtze, shot by the Japanese, or trampled to death by their comrades attempting to force their way out of the single gate not yet in Japanese hands. Some 70,000 men of the Nationalist army lost their lives in the Battle of Nanking. Tang himself escaped in a coal-driven boat with a few of his leading officers.

The Japanese hoped the Chinese would surrender following the loss of their capital. Instead, Chiang Kai-Shek issued a fire-breathing statement widely distributed in China, which, in large measure, struck exactly the chord the Nationalist leader hoped it would:

"'The war will not be decided in Nanking or any other city,' he said. 'It will be decided in the countryside of our vast country and by the inflexible will of our people. We shall fight on every step of the way, and every inch of the 40,000,000 square *li* of our territory.'" (Taylor, 2009, 152).

China, as Chiang Kai-Shek hoped, would fight on against the Japanese, though the Nationalist cause suffered a serious blow from the decimation of its soldiery. However, the date also marked the beginning of one of history's most concentrated atrocities.

## Chapter 4: The Start of the Nanking Massacre

The Japanese showed a profound lack of understanding of human psychology during their advance after the seizure of Shanghai, compounded by a Bushido ethic and sense of racial superiority that together gave license – in fact, extreme encouragement – to sadistic brutality and murderous impulses. They believed that killing and torturing the Chinese in vast numbers would cow the rest into submission.

**Japanese Soldiers Marching to Nanking**

Instead, their deeds predictably produced rage, hatred, and iron determination in their adversaries, and united disparate Chinese factions with a shared resolve to resist the Japanese and make their conquest of China as difficult and costly as possible.

Nevertheless, the Japanese never grasped this fundamental and fairly evident truth. Chinese intransigence in the face of Japanese brutality simply led the Japanese to believe they had not used *enough* cruelty and caused them to expand the butchery further. In the primly evasive phrase of Emperor Hirohito, the Japanese wanted these measures to produce "self-reflection" among the Chinese.

While Japanese leaders gave no specific order for the Nanking Massacre, they explicitly commanded the literal extermination of the Chinese peasantry during the march from Shanghai to Nanking:

> "All the law-abiding people have retreated within the walls. Treat everyone found outside the walls as anti-Japanese and destroy them. [...] Since it is convenient in conducting sweep operations to burn down houses, prepare materials." (Bix, 2000, 333).

The Japanese 10th Army carried out these orders assiduously, giving a preview of the hecatomb to follow once Nanking fell. The Japanese soldiers shot Chinese military prisoners *en masse*, or, in a number of cases, roped large numbers of wounded Chinese together, drenched them in gasoline, and set them on fire to burn agonizingly alive. They also burned down every village and small city they encountered and raped practically every woman or female child seized.

Panicked masses of Chinese farmers and townspeople flowed across the landscape ahead of the Japanese advance, desperately seeking escape. Many sought refuge inside Nanking, destined to become a trap where tens of thousands of them would die lingering, painful deaths and then be discarded in the river or "Trenches of Ten Thousand Corpses."

These actions represented no anomaly from historic Japanese behavior. Though Bushido represented a code of "honor" in the same way as European chivalry, its focus remained tremendously different. The chivalric codes of Europe contained injunctions to spare (or even defend) the weak and defenseless, to show mercy to prisoners and the wounded, and so forth. Though flouted at times, these codes slowly evolved into the later code of "gentleman's warfare" and eventually into the Geneva Convention, which effectively remains the chivalric code in an updated, legalistic format.

Bushido, on the other hand, emphasized success as honorable and failure as dishonorable, which explains why defeated Japanese, for centuries, committed seppuku rather than survive in "shame." The dark corollary of this grim practice expressed itself in active hatred and aggression towards those who would not or could not fight. Not merely dismissed as "unworthy," they drew venomous loathing from the Japanese under arms.

To the Japanese, the concepts of an honorably defeated prisoner or a noncombatant did not exist. A fighting man who, outnumbered, exhausted, wounded, and hopeless, chose to surrender did not represent a fellow warrior deserving a measure of sympathy for misfortune due to circumstances far beyond his individual control. He represented, instead, a loathsome criminal and a sort of traitor to the concept of the fighting man, deserving punishment for not killing himself in defeat.

Worse, this loathing extended to noncombatants; the Japanese, preparing for the invasion of the home islands by the Americans in 1945, trained their children in the thousands to use grenades so that they could pull the pin, walk up to Americans, and detonate the weapon, killing themselves and perhaps one or more soldiers as well.

The reflexes of Bushido trained men to see even a civilian who failed to immolate themselves for their nation as a sort of abomination, a renegade deserving only contempt, pain, and death. This frenzied code produced a capacity for boundless cruelty without remorse or any kind of introspection, particularly when coupled with the fascist-style nationalism of the 20th century Japanese military.

Almost precisely the same behavior manifested itself during the Japanese invasion of Korea in 1592, some 350 years earlier. The Japanese samurai acted the same as their remote descendants in Nanking, killing tens of thousands of civilians, committing mass torture and mass rape, burning countless buildings, and time and again showing in their own accounts evidence of a deep relish and pleasure derived from witnessing the torment and killing of thousands of other human beings:

> "Some Japanese accounts note the taking of 20,000 heads at Chinju. Korean records claim 60,000 deaths, and both figures imply a massacre of soldiers and non-combatants alike. [...] That night, while the Nam river downstream from the castle walls flowed red, and headless corpses still choked its banks, the victorious Japanese generals celebrated in the Ch'oksongnu Pavilion, from which the best view of this hellish scene could be appreciated." (Turnbull, 2002, 160).

Japanese scroll paintings and woodcuts of the 1592 invasion frankly include numerous scenes eerily reminiscent of the horrors photographed by stunned foreigners in Nanking three and a half centuries later: soldiers cutting down fleeing, screaming civilians and setting fire to their homes, grinning soldiers dragging women away to be raped, female corpses sprawled on the ground with their skirts ominously pulled up to expose their lower bodies, presumably indicating the Japanese raped and then murdered them.

The Japanese cut off 214,752 heads during their invasion, not counting those discarded as being of "low quality," and shipped an additional 38,000 Korean noses, severed and pickled, back to Japan as a trophy. The Japanese buried these pitiful remnants in the misnamed

"Mimizuka," or "Ear Mound," which still stands in Kyoto. The Shogun Toyotomi Hideyoshi gave orders to his samurai which would have fit naturally with the men who committed the Nanking Massacre twelve generations later:

> "Mow down everyone universally, without discriminating between young and old, men and women, clergy and the laity – high ranking soldiers on the battlefield, that goes without saying, but also the hill folk, down to the poorest and meanest – and send the heads to Japan." (Hawley, 2005, 465-466).

A gentle and humane Japanese Buddhist monk named Keinen accompanied Hideyoshi's expedition, and recorded an endless catalog of horrors. He saw men and women tortured and killed in front of their children, workmen beaten to death, samurai butchering villagers, and countless slaves led away in iron and bamboo collars.

He also walked through towns and into the countryside beyond and found the ground carpeted for some distance with the mutilated corpses of slaughtered Koreans that he could not, in his own words, "force himself to look at." Finally, in despair, he attempted to sum up his feelings with a stark phrase suitable for the epitaph of Nanking centuries after his death, as the samurai of another age spread similar desolation in China: "Hell cannot be in any other place except here." (Turnbull, 2002, 206).

In a real sense, the soldiers who raped, tortured, and killed hundreds of thousands of civilians in Nanking simply carried on the long-standing traditions of samurai warfare. Some Japanese, of course, remained untouched by this brutal code of "honor" and showed compassion. But in the Rape of Nanking, their numbers proved to be a very small minority, to the misfortune of those caught in the Japanese Army's clutches.

## Chapter 5: Foreigners Prepare the Safety Zone

Very few foreigners remained in Nanking at the time of its fall, but that tiny handful made a tremendous difference in the outcome. Many more Chinese would likely have died without these courageous two dozen Europeans, who enjoyed nearly complete immunity due to the Japanese wish to avoid bringing the wrath of the western powers down on their heads at this crucial juncture.

The majority of this group consisted of Americans, and since at this point the United States still supplied many materials to the Japanese, killing or detaining these people would be impolitic at best and disastrous at worst. Most participated in missionary work, while one, John Rabe, represented the German Siemens company in the city and performed many acts of heroic kindness despite his status as an avowed Nazi (albeit one focusing almost exclusively on the "socialist" aspects of the NSDAP rather than on its militant or racist facets).

As the Japanese pushed the Nationalists out of Shanghai, the foreigners banded together to create a "Safety Zone" in the western quadrant of the city. At this point, they feared violence and rape from Chiang Kai-Shek's nationalist soldiers, disorganized and undisciplined following defeat, as the missionaries imagined them. Naively, they imagined that the Safety Zone would exist for only a few days, providing the local Chinese with shelter from their compatriots under arms. Then, when the civilized, honorable, and disciplined Japanese arrived, the foreigners could allow everyone to return home safely.

Though the exact opposite of reality – the Chinese soldiers proved too busy fighting for their lives to create the type of mayhem feared, and still retained some of their discipline, while the Japanese approached along roads they strewed with raped and shattered bodies – this scenario at least served to motivate the foreigners to prepare the Safety Zone quickly and thoroughly before the Japanese entered the city:

> "Indeed, one of the foreign eyewitnesses of the 1937 massacre admitted: "We were more prepared for excesses from the fleeing Chinese... but never, never from the Japanese. On the contrary, we had expected that with the appearance of the Japanese the return of peace, quiet, and prosperity would occur." (Chang, 1997, 83).

Many foreigners fled immediately before fighting reached Nanking, leaving only a resolute core of those willing to help in any way they could. Some of the last to escape prior to the Rape left on American gunboats. One of these, the *Panay*, suffered the grimly ironic fate of sinking at the hands of Japanese pilots – its occupants would actually have found more safety in the city they abandoned than in the vessel in which they departed.

Attacking an American gunboat represented a stark departure from overall Japanese policy at the time, which generally treated all European and American foreigners as sacrosanct. Unusually for a military establishment where questioning an order frequently led to summary execution, the Japanese pilots protested the orders to attack the *Panay* repeatedly and vehemently.

Only after several rounds of threats from their officers did they reluctantly bomb and strafe the vessel. This appears to be an indication that a splinter, reckless military faction actually ordered the attack, rather than the main command structure.

The remaining group consisted of 17 U.S. citizens, six Germans, two Russians, a Britisher, and an Austrian. These men and women devised the idea of a Safety Zone in November, approximately a month before the Japanese took the city, and organized themselves into the International Committee for the Nanking Safety Zone during their first official meeting on November 22nd, 1937. At this gathering, the 27 Committee members also elected John Rabe as their chairman.

Rabe, a small, bald, bespectacled man with a thick cookie duster mustache and a disarming sense of humor alongside an explosive temper when confronted by injustice or disorder, had returned to the city to represent Siemens' interests and look after his own property when he learned of Japanese bombing. He stated in his diary that he had no wish to die for either, but felt he could not leave the city anyway: "Under such circumstances, can I, may I, cut and run? I don't think so. Anyone who has ever sat in a dugout and held a trembling Chinese child in each hand through the long hours of an air raid can understand what I feel." (Rabe, 1998, 5).

Rabe began his humanitarian work in Nanking in an effort to help his 30 Chinese servants, most of whose homes lay in the Japanese-controlled north and who could not now return home through the fighting lines. He made a primitive dugout to shelter from shrapnel during air raids, stocked food and water, and even prepared vinegar masks to try to preserve his life and the lives of his employees if the Japanese used poison gas. As it happened, the Japanese used gas 13 times during the Battle of Nanking, but abandoned the practice long before the city fell because the vapors frequently blew back into their lines and killed many of their own soldiers.

Rabe also painted a huge swastika on a piece of canvas 20 feet across and placed it flat on the ground outside his house, so that the Japanese pilots would hopefully identify it as a German residence and refrain from bombing it. With unintentional understatement – considering that the Safety Zone might have saved as many as 50,000 lives – Rabe reported tersely on his November 22nd election as Committee chairman:

"Five p.m. meeting of the International Committee for Establishing a Neutral Zone for Noncombatants in Nanking. They elect me chairman. My protests are to no avail. I give in for the sake of a good cause. I hope I prove worthy of the post, which can very well become important." (Rabe, 1998, 27).

As the Japanese began their attack, all of the Chinese residents with enough money to flee left the city, leaving behind the poorest people to suffer whatever fate might bring them. Rabe, confronted by a Nationalist colonel named Huang who berated him for creating a Safety Zone when the remaining civilians, trapped with nowhere to go, might otherwise be coerced into aiding his soldiers, asked in disgust why the rich always demand that those most unfortunate in life serve as martyrs to their country while the affluent escape, heaping scorn on those who die for them.

The International Committee worked feverishly to set up the Safety Zone with whatever materials they could access. The Zone covered a significant area in the western part of Nanking, forming a stretched hexagon bounded by major roads – North Chungshan Road on the north, Chung Yang Road on the east, Hanchung Road on the south, and part of Haikang Road on the west.

The Zone included the American, German, and Japanese embassies, several missionary-operated universities including the University of Nanking, the Drum Tower Hospital, and the Army Staff College, all of which provided important indoor spaces to the Committee. These large public buildings soon served as hospitals, food storage and distribution points, administrative centers, and occasional refuges for the most vulnerable people to seek sanctuary inside the Safety Zone.

Luckily, missionary work and business experience gave the odd assemblage of foreigners on the International Committee the drive and organizational ability necessary to put together a massive, if basic, rescue scheme on a very tight schedule. Using university-educated Chinese as their lieutenants, the Committee members demarcated the Safety Zone's boundaries with numerous flags, many laid flat on rooftops or the ground so that Japanese airmen could clearly see the Zone's edges.

Helpers put up posters in Chinese throughout the city, urging residents and refugees alike to gather inside the Safety Zone. This soon produced a flood of thousands of people trying to find safety for themselves and their families. The organizers sent their limited supply of trucks throughout the city, collecting rice and other food stores abandoned by the Chinese military, along with medicine and other vital supplies.

The International Committee also contacted the headquarters of the Japanese 10th Army and requested that the soldiers of the Empire of Japan refrain from shelling or bombing the Zone. The Japanese, mostly because they wished to avoid killing foreigners and thus turn the western powers against them, agreed, and largely respected this agreement. However, the Safety Zone eventually proved somewhat less safe than hoped.

John Rabe had only slight faith in the Japanese promises not to shell the Zone. However, with characteristic humor, he took advantage of his own fears to include a wryly jocular entry in his diary on December 11th, referencing his pet bird, Peter: "Water and electricity are off. The bombardment continues. Now and then the noise     ebbs a bit, only to break out anew. Our Peter appears to love it. He sings along at full      throat. Canaries apparently have better nerves than a Rabe." (Rabe, 1998, 60).

Despite the Committee's efforts to disarm them or clear them out entirely, armed Chinese soldiers from the Nationalist forces remained inside the Safety Zone. Their presence caused immense alarm to the organizers, who feared the Japanese would simply launch a full-scale military attack and mow down everyone in their attempt to kill the soldiers using the Zone as "cover." However, they still expected the Japanese to behave in accordance with the laws of war and the Safety Zone to be needed only briefly. The first entry of Japanese troops into Nanking disabused them of these high-flown expectations abruptly and shockingly.

The sound of gunfire accompanied the entry of the Japanese into Nanking – not the back-and-forth exchange of firefights between attackers and defenders, since the Chinese soldiery no longer resisted at that point, but the slowly spreading discharges of death squads mowing down randomly encountered people in the streets.

When the Japanese moved forward to take the metropolis, some of the half-million resident Chinese remaining within its walls actually ran out the gates to welcome them. They met with a very different reception than they expected from the victorious Imperial Japanese Army (IJA). Estimates put the number of people shot within the first two days of Nanking's fall at between 7,000 and 12,000, most gunned down casually by troops moving to take up positions assigned to them in the city's districts.

Eyewitnesses reported seeing many corpses lying along the streets with gunshot wounds in their backs as people, realizing the nature of their new masters, vainly attempted to flee the men Chiang Kai-Shek characterized as "dwarf bandits." The vanguard consisted of the 6th and 116th Infantry Divisions, supported by the 16th Division, which entered via the Taiping and Zhongshan Gates, and the 9th Division, marching through the Guanghua Gate.

While the Japanese initially avoided mass murder inside the Safety Zone, soldiers entered it almost immediately to loot and commit rape. Even in the first few days, some Chinese men in the Zone died to IJA bullets when they attempted to keep their wives, sisters, or daughters from suffering rape. Lewis Smythe, Secretary of the International Committee, wrote a long list of grievances to Japanese command, including this item:

> "On the night of December 14, there were many cases of Japanese soldiers entering Chinese houses and raping women or taking them away. This created a panic in the area and hundreds of women moved into the Ginling College campus yesterday. Consequently, three American men spent the night at Ginling College last night to protect the 3,000 women and children in the compound." (Brook, 1999, 10).

These actions – including random bayoneting and shooting of Chinese men – created an immediate crisis. Many of the Committee's Chinese helpers refused to go outside to prepare and distribute rice to the refugees, fearing murder by the prowling Japanese. With just 27 foreigners – able to move freely without risk of attack – in total, feeding thousands of refugees immediately grew into an insurmountable problem.

Predictably, worse soon followed. To provide some security for the Safety Zone, the International Committee organized Chinese volunteers into a temporary, unarmed police force. The Japanese targeted these men next, as John Rabe explained in a polite but deeply indignant letter to the IJA command on December 17th:

"Our police were interfered with and yesterday 50 of them stationed at the Ministry of Justice were marched off, 'to be killed' according to the Japanese officer in charge, and yesterday afternoon 46 of our 'volunteer police' were similarly marched off. [...] These 'volunteer police' were neither uniformed nor armed in any way. They simply wore our armbands. They were more like Boy Scouts in the West who do odd jobs in helping to keep crowds in order, clean up, and render first aid, etc." (Brook, 1999, 14).

Trying to keep their charges alive, the westerners of the International Committee used the private cars at their disposal to distribute as much food as possible to the Chinese cowering indoors, fearing to emerge into the streets where Japanese soldiers prowled, looking for items to steal and women to rape.

General Matsui Iwane, the 10th Army commander, only entered the city on December 17th, riding on horseback and accompanied by an escorting unit of cavalry for his grand entrance. Matsui remained for only five days before returning to Shanghai on December 22nd, 1937.

**Matsui Iwane**

The general later sanctimoniously claimed ignorance of the incident, while simultaneously and rather contradictorily asserting he dressed down Prince Akaga and other field commanders for "abominable incidents" lasting "50 days" in Nanking. This, of course, begs the question why Matsui, if truly as outraged as he claimed, failed to return even once to Nanking to halt the massacre, or even attempt to halt it.

Even if Matsui did, in fact, verbally assail his subordinates over the ongoing slaughter and mass rape, he never issued a written order to stop or even condemn it. His admission that he knew of the Rape of Nanking and his indisputable inaction (at the very least) in failing to deal with it sufficed for the Allied war crimes judges after the war, who sentenced him to hang.

Though the Japanese soldiers began an orgy of looting, rape, torture, and mass murder immediately after their arrival, they did not run amok in the usual understanding of the word. They remained highly organized, showing that military discipline and chain of command still operated to the full. In fact, many of the atrocities could not have occurred without large-scale coordination and careful planning, enabling the efficient movement of large numbers of prisoners to killing sites, the disposal of bodies, and so on.

Even more starkly, the immunity enjoyed by the tiny handful of Americans, Germans, and other European foreigners amid the khaki ocean of the Japanese 10th Army demonstrates incontrovertibly that the chain of command remained intact and the officer corps maintained iron control throughout the Massacre. The members of the International Committee photographed and filmed the horrors taking place, berated and harassed Japanese soldiers engaged in war crimes, and sometimes even physically intervened to prevent rapes. Yet not one died, or even suffered a wound, at the hands of the soldiers.

This is not to say the Japanese soldiers participated unwillingly. On the contrary, most appeared eager to let loose the inmost appetites of the human animal. In the words of one Japanese medical corps Staff Sergeant, "The soldiers practically fell over themselves rushing to gang rape [the women]" (Honda, 2015, 120). However, those appetites, aggressions, and impulses operated only within precise boundaries set by the military authorities, and the survival of the meddling, isolated band of 27 foreigners in their midst through the whole six weeks of incessant slaughter underlines how scrupulously every soldier stayed within those boundaries, set by higher authority.

These facts strongly belie later claims by the Japanese officers that they lost control over their men and had no ability whatsoever to influence events. In fact, both officers and soldiers wanted precisely the same thing, and each cooperated fully in their role in carrying out what stands as probably history's largest single-location war crime.

## Chapter 7: The Rape of Nanking

The Japanese carried out wholesale extermination attempts on the male population of

Nanking, likely killing well over 200,000 men in total. Most of these victims consisted of civilians, though prisoners of war and unarmed military deserters trying to hide in the local population also suffered destruction. A Japanese woman attached to a "Pacification Unit" later wrote about one of the many techniques used to kill men in large numbers:

> "Both men and women were stripped naked and made to march single file. The Japanese soldiers assembled on each side of the road, applauding and having a great time as they watched. The men were driven into the river, and as each one's head broke through to the water's surface, he was shot and killed right there. It's not hard to imagine how the remaining women were treated." (Honda, 2015, 121).

Shooting men in the Yangtze River solved the problem of corpse disposal also, since the stream carried away most of the cadavers. However, this represented only one of the many methods the IJA soldiery used in committing mass murder, as documented in excruciating detail both by foreign eyewitnesses and by numerous accounts and photographs generated by the Japanese themselves.

In some areas, the Japanese engaged in "beheading training," using samurai swords and other bladed weapons to sever the necks of numerous Chinese men. These massacres took place systematically next to huge open pits dug beforehand to receive the corpses. The Japanese roped the Chinese men together in long rows, then moved systematically down the line, chopping off heads and rolling the corpses into the mass graves.

Some Chinese escaped death when the Japanese, exhausted by the hard physical work of butchering thousands of human beings, substituted stabbing for decapitation. This allowed a few Chinese to throw themselves into the pit and sham death until the Japanese left, then crawl out and escape, fleeing into the countryside or to the Safety Zone.

**Japanese Soldiers Searching Chinese for Weapons**

The Japanese also used tens of thousands of Chinese men for live bayonet practice. The soldiers forced Chinese to dig wide, shallow ditches, then herded their victims into the ditch with their hands pinioned behind their backs. Japanese soldiers carrying rifles with fixed bayonets then entered the ditch and practiced various close combat attacks on their helpless prisoners.

Photographs of these scenes survive. In one example, the photographer captured the moment when one Japanese soldier stabs a man who is apparently sinking down and dying. A second Japanese jabs his bayonet into the abdomen of a prone form, apparently already dead or nearly so. In the foreground, a third IJA soldier is making a violent underarm thrust at a man curled up defensively against the wall of the trench, trying vainly to fend off the bayonet with his bare foot.

Other Chinese died even more slowly. The Japanese bound groups of men hand and foot and buried them alive. In other cases, they buried the victims up to their necks, then ran their heads over with tanks or armored cars. In several cases, seeking sadistic entertainment, IJA soldiers buried groups of naked Chinese men up to their waists in the ground and then loosed attack-trained German shepherds on the victims. Half-buried, the men could not escape, but with their arms still free, they could attempt – vainly – to fend off the dogs, which ripped out their throats or disemboweled them.

In other cases, the Japanese soaked crowds of bound men in gasoline and either set them afire directly or shot them with machine guns, the tracer rounds setting the gasoline alight. So many corpses were collected that disposal became a massive problem, and the air filled with an overwhelming stench of decaying flesh even in winter. Photographs show heaps of dead bodies on the Yangtze shore and giant mass graves. Once the river froze over, the Japanese trucked corpses out onto the ice, cut large holes in the surface, and dumped their ghastly cargo through to be swept away downstream.

Thousands of other men died individually in casual killings or, very frequently, when they tried to defend their families from rape. Murder of a household's male inhabitants often served as a prelude to gang-rapes of its women. A few Japanese even reportedly cut off and ate the penises of Chinese men they killed, believing this would increase their sexual prowess and overall virility.

In other cases, the Japanese kept victims alive for extended torture. Soon after the occupation began, the soldiers stripped hundreds of men and women naked, tied them to the pillars in a university building, and probed their bodies with sharpened awls, inflicting hundreds of wounds on each. A number of observers, both foreign and Chinese, reported on incidents where the Japanese suspended prisoners – both men and women – by hooks driven through their tongues, then watched the agonized struggles of the victims.

Some of the Japanese expressed shock and amazement when first confronted by the outpouring of violence. One officer named Tominaga Shozo, arriving on the scene fresh from the academy, felt a measure of alarm when he first got a close look at the men the Army assigned him to command: "They had evil eyes," he remembered. "They weren't human eyes, but the eyes of     leopards or tigers." (Chang, 1997, 48).

Officers made sure to harden such men to killing quickly by ordering them to bayonet or behead terrified prisoners. Many, already fully indoctrinated by the militaristic culture and a contempt for their own lives that made them value those of other people even less, adapted almost instantly to the grisly sport. While Tominaga Shozo stated it took three months for him to become a "demon," other men like Nagatomi Hakudo readily admitted to exulting in killing almost from the first:

"The Japanese officer [...] unsheathed his sword, spat on it, and with a sudden mighty
    swing he brought it down on the neck of a Chinese boy cowering before us. The   head was cut clean off and tumbled away [...] as the body slumped forward, blood       spurting in two great gushing fountains from the neck. The officer suggested I take     the head home as a souvenir. I remember smiling proudly as I took his sword and       began killing people." (Chang, 1997, 49).

Nagatomi, never punished for his crimes, later became a doctor and, when asked, stated that he murdered approximately 200 prisoners personally during his time in Nanking, using beheading, live burial, and burning alive. While the Japanese killed the largest portion of the men in the first week or two of occupation, thousands more murders and executions – often carried out in extremely torturous fashion – continued throughout the entire six-week period of the Massacre.

Amid a sea of slaughter so vast its perpetrators frequently blend into an anonymous, bloodthirsty collective, at least one incident stands out sharply as the handiwork of two identifiable individuals. The so-called "Contest to Cut Down a Hundred" between two second lieutenants appeared in a series of articles printed in the Tokyo Nichinichi Shimbun newspaper in late 1937, detailing the supposed "heroic" deeds of the "contestants."

Noda Tsuyoshi and Mukai Toshiaki, two second lieutenants, began a "contest" to see who could kill 100 Chinese first. The newspapers reported the grisly affair as occurring in the thick of battle:

> "As Second Lieutenant M[ukai], who has reached the third *dan* in bayonet training, runs his fingers over the blade of "Seki-no-Magoroku," the sword at his side, Second Lieutenant N[oda] speaks of his treasured sword [...] On the day after their separate departures, Second Lieutenant N[oda] broke into an enemy pillbox [and] killed four enemy [...] Second Lieutenant M[ukai] invaded an enemy camp at Henglinzhen [...] and laid fifty-five enemy low with his sword." (Honda, 2015, 125).

**A Japanese Story Describing the "Contest"**

The incident highlights the incredible levels of jingoism inculcated into the Japanese of the era by their government, and the underdevelopment of critical thinking skills even in those otherwise well-educated by Imperial universities. Most Japanese interpreted the contest as meaning the second lieutenants charged heroically in amongst the Chinese enemy and cut down dozens like action movie samurai.

No such action could in fact occur. The Nationalist soldiers, well-armed with high powered rifles generally maintained better than their owners, would inevitably have killed a lone man with a sword attempting to close to melee range. Even if trained to standards inferior to those used for Japanese soldiers, the idea of a swordsman plowing through trenches or camps filled with hostile riflemen and leaving "red ruin" in his wake appears ludicrous and impossible.

Noda himself scoffed at the notion when he spoke at the school in his hometown and frankly admitted to committing mass murder of helpless prisoners. After declaring "that stuff in the newspapers about the 'brave warrior from the provinces' and the 'brave warrior of contest to cut down a hundred,' that's me," he described how once a band of Chinese soldiers surrendered to the Japanese:

"We'd line them up and cut them down, from one end of the line to the other. I was praised for having killed a hundred people, but actually, almost all of them were killed in this way. The two of us did have a contest, but afterward, I was often asked whether it was a big deal, and I said that it was no big deal." (Honda, 2015, 126).

The heroism, in fact, consisted of plain butchery. Since both men passed 100 "kills" and remained uncertain who "scored" the highest first, they went into what the newspapers called "extra innings" to see who could reach 150 first.

The newspaper clippings later proved the two officers' doom. Presented at trial as evidence of war crimes, the articles assured Mukai's and Noda's condemnation to death, a verdict greeted by a round of spontaneous, enthusiastic applause in the Chinese postwar courtroom. The Chinese executed the two lieutenants by firing squad.

Accompanying the endless scenes of butchery that choked every street and alley in the city with bloated, reeking corpses, the Japanese raped nearly every woman they could catch. While naturally giving preference to young, attractive women, the soldiers raped females of every age, including the very old and the very young. The IJA soldiery raped at least 80,000 women. Many of these unfortunates suffered violation dozens of times. In a number of cases, so many men raped women in succession that they ruptured the women's genital area in the process, causing them to bleed to death.

The Japanese soldiers usually killed any men present before or after the rapes, particularly if the Chinese dared to attempt fighting off the rapists, who typically moved in bands of 20 to 30 to ensure their ability to overwhelm any opposition. At other times, however, the IJA soldiers amused themselves by forcing men to rape their relatives, such as making fathers rape their daughters or sons rape their mothers while the Japanese watched. Many Chinese refused, resulting in their immediate murder by the troops. At least one family committed mass suicide by leaping into the Yangtze and drowning rather than submit to raping one another.

While most rapes involved men raping women, some of the Japanese soldiers also raped Chinese men. A variant on the theme involved forcing Chinese men to rape each other under threat of immediate execution in the case of non-compliance. The Japanese also sodomized men with foreign objects, often inflicting fatal injuries in the process.

When the rapes usually ended with the murder of the women involved. Frequently, the killing of the women involved the most gruesome kinds of torture. A favorite method of executing a rape victim involved shoving a long sharpened bamboo stake, a cane, a bayonet, or another sharp foreign object into her vagina, causing her to die from internal injuries. Several photographs of female bodies in this condition survive, in one case with a Japanese soldier standing calmly next to the corpse.

In other cases, the soldiers stuffed live grenades or lit firecrackers into the victim's vagina to kill her. Many others simply died under a flurry of bayonet thrusts or received the relative mercy of shooting. However, the soldiers often seemed to be on the lookout for sadistic ways to increase their victim's suffering with an agonizing death following the shock and horror of violation, as a medical officer later confessed:

"There was a girl – she may have waited too long to flee – who had blackened her face and put on men's clothes and waded into the river to hide. The soldiers pulled her out of the river and made her rinse herself off... The way it ended was that they tied her hands, shoved her into a shed that had straw piled up around it, and burned her to death." (Honda, 2015, 120).

The Japanese raped female children and sometimes infants also. If the act proved impossible initially for physical reasons, the soldiers simply sliced the victim's genital area open with a bayonet before committing the rape. Frequently, soldiers killed a woman's child first before raping her. Others slashed open the stomachs of pregnant women and extracted the fetuses to kill separately before leaving the woman to die of her injuries. One Japanese sergeant later left a harrowing account:

"I took a living human child, that is, an innocent baby that was just beginning to talk, and threw it into boiling water. When the mother, desperate to save her child, rushed over to the kettle, I sneered contemptuously and said, 'If you take care of the brat, you'll be next, and I'll do it slowly.' Then I kicked her in the abdomen so she went flying." (Honda, 2015, 121).

Other women became sex slaves for the conquering Japanese, their degradation continuing for the entire period of the Massacre or in some cases longer. At the bottom of this ghastly hierarchy of victims existed women turned into a sort of "rape furniture," tied naked to posts or bed frames at the entrances to barracks or inside the barracks themselves. Left in these exposed positions for extended periods of time, these women remained available for casual rape by any passing Japanese who randomly felt the urge to violate them. Once damaged or otherwise rendered less attractive, the Japanese often killed them and replaced them with other victims.

The Japanese soldiers also objected to washing their own garments, so the Army gathered large numbers of women to serve as laundry slaves. Kept prisoner near barracks and other facilities, these women scrubbed uniforms clean by day, then suffered sexual assault at night for the entertainment of their captors. As a letter from Dr. Robert O. Wilson of the University

Hospital, an American, to the Japanese authorities described, speaking of one such incident:

"They were taken by Japanese soldiers to a location in the west central portion of the    city where from the activity she judged there was a Japanese military hospital. The    women washed clothes during the day and were raped throughout the night. The    older ones were being raped from 10 to 20 times, the younger and good looking ones    as many as 40 times a night." (Brook, 1999, 65).

The Japanese forced the most attractive women into service as "comfort women" in early examples of their infamous "comfort stations." Though generally not raped to death, and very seldom bayoneted or shot, these women remained as sexual captives for years – permanent slaves meant to satisfy the lusts of Japanese soldiers stationed in the city or moving through it on their way to other postings.

Those women not killed outright during or immediately after rape often found themselves pregnant with a half-Japanese child. Many women killed these infants immediately after their birth. Others, when they realized their pregnancy, committed suicide by leaping from rooftops or drowning themselves in the Yangtze, joining those who killed themselves due to being unable to cope with the emotional devastation following sexual assault. A few carried their babies to term and then raised them, but often remained conflicted and tormented for years about their choice.

Though hampered by their low numbers and lack of any effective power beyond that offered by courage and a sense of moral duty, the foreign members of the International Committee for the Safety Zone did their best to ameliorate the horrors around them. When they could not, they used still cameras and, in the case of the missionary John Magee, an early motion picture camera, to document as much of the mayhem and slaughter as possible for eventual war crimes prosecution.

The Committee members worked hard to keep people inside the Safety Zone safe from execution or kidnapping. They also sought to prevent rapes, though the Japanese frequently broke into houses or dormitories at night and raped dozens of women anyway. Using the medical supplies gathered, they treated hundreds of victims with bayonet or bullet wounds, sword wounds, or genitals mangled by mass gang-rape. They also kept thousands alive by organizing relief kitchens and providing rice meals on a daily basis, sometimes supplemented with fish or chicken when they could buy these meats.

Medical care and food – often prepared and distributed by Chinese assistants to John Rabe's "Red Swastika" branch, the Nazi equivalent of the Red Cross – accounted for most of the help the Committee could provide to the people of Nanking. By their count, approximately 49,000 to 51,000 people sheltered inside the Safety Zone. While not immune to rape and murder, these individuals experienced less violence than those in the city and its suburbs, and received regular food from the huge kitchens organized by the missionaries, doctors, and businesspeople.

These individuals at least owed their survival mainly to the International Committee, due to immense food scarcity in the city.

These brave men and women also protested constantly – though futility – to the Japanese authorities, sending countless letters describing rape, pillage, and murder. Courteously but insistently, they demanded redress, though of course the IJA made no effort to oblige.

On some occasions, the foreigners managed to intervene in an individual rape or killing and save the victim. They could do nothing, of course, for those rounded up for mass torture and execution, where thousands of Japanese soldiers acted in concert under the command of their officers. John Rabe managed on several occasions to overawe potential rapists by displaying the emblem of Nazi Germany, Japan's ally:

"Six Japanese climbed over my garden wall and attempted to open the gates from the inside. When I arrive and shine my flashlight in the face of one of the bandits, he reaches for his pistol, but his hand drops quickly enough when I yell at him and hold my swastika armband under his nose. Then, on my orders, all six have to scramble back over the wall. My gates will never be opened to riffraff like that " (Rabe, 1998, 34).

The Japanese excluded other foreigners from entering the city also. Diplomatic representatives of America and Germany naturally wished to learn the fate and situation of their citizens in Nanking, but the IJA maintained close control on all movements into and out of the city, as noted in the diary of Tsen Shui-Feng, the Chinese assistant of Minnie Vautrin, a missionary who undertook organizing the protection, feeding, and medical treatment of women and children in the Safety Zone:

"The Americans requested the Japanese consul to telegram Shanghai for more manpower to help here. They refused. They deliberately did so. The German consul at Hsia Kwan is not allowed to enter the city [...] He [the Japanese consul] wants neither the third country [Germany] to see their immoral deeds, nor people to see the corpses lying on the roads. Some of the roads, [people] can only see dead bodies, but not the road." (Hu, 2010, 99).

The Japanese refused to allow additional foreigners to enter the city until the spring of 1938, by which time they concealed much of the evidence of massacre through burial and cremation. During the worst of the mayhem, a news blackout by the Imperial occupiers effectively concealed the extent and savagery of the destruction from the outside world.

After the first month of terror and destruction, the Rape of Nanking's fury slowly ebbed. Murder, torture, rape, looting, and arson continued well into January 1938, but at a declining rate. Miner Searle Bates, a university historian, highlighted the reason for this in a letter sent to unspecified acquaintances in the United States:

"Dear Friends: – A few hasty jottings amid rape and bayonet stabs and reckless
shooting, to be sent on the first foreign boat available since the situation    developed
after the Japanese entry – a U.S. Navy tug [...] Things have eased a good   deal since New Year
within the crowded Safety Zone, largely through the departure      of the main hordes of
soldiers." (Kaiyuan, 2001, 14).

The behavior of the Japanese soldiers underwent little change but their numbers dwindled
as the Tenth Army shifted south for new campaigns (and brought massacre and mass rape to new
towns, villages, and regions). On January 1st, 1938, the Japanese established a puppet
government made up of Chinese under Japanese military authority, the Nanjing Zizhi
Weiyuanhui, or Nanking Self-Government Committee.

The new Chinese government proved a mixed blessing. The officials themselves lost no
time in enrichment through plunder, adding to the problems of a city already picked clean with
vulture-like efficiency by the Japanese. However, they also did much to restore the metropolis to
some sort of working order. The deep drifts of garbage and shredded, putrid human flesh which
the Japanese left in the roads, killing anyone who dared to attempt cleanup, now underwent
removal under the Zizhi Weiyuanhui's supervision.

Within a month, the city once again enjoyed electricity, running water, and ricksha and
bus services. The stench of death lingered but slowly abated. The Japanese, whose garrison
ceased random killings once the Tenth Army left, established shops to exploit the population
(whose own stores the Japanese earlier destroyed systematically), and built opium dens
throughout the city. The misery of their situation prompted people to grasp at the brief respite
drugs offered: "To encourage addiction and further enslave the people, the Japanese routinely
used    narcotics as payment for labor and prostitution in Nanking. Heroin cigarettes were
offered to children as young as ten. Based on his research [...] Miner Searle Bates
concluded that some fifty thousand people in the Nanking area were using heroin—
one-eighth of the population at the time."

Chinese workers in Japanese factories received pay but also suffered frequent abuse, up
to and including execution by torture for minor thefts. The infamous Unit 731, which carried out
lethal medical experiments on living human beings, opened a heavily guarded facility in
Nanking. Here, anyone accused of minor infractions against Japanese regulations might find
themselves dissected alive, infected with fatal disease organisms and left untreated, or subjected
to a range of agonizing, grotesque medical experiments, before being dumped into the facility's
incinerator.

Nevertheless, Nanking rebounded once massacre and random killing in the streets ceased.
Though oppressed and tormented for the remainder of the war, the Chinese population of the city
managed to restore a semblance of normal life and carry on agricultural and economic activity, a
striking testament to human resiliency.

## Chapter 8: Postwar Justice and War Crimes Trials

When the Japanese evacuated the city in 1945, following the American atomic bombing of Nagasaki and Hiroshima, very few reprisals occurred against them by the Chinese despite the defeat of the Empire of the Rising Sun. Thoroughly terrorized and cowed by Japanese brutality, the Chinese mostly hid themselves in their houses for several days, emerging to find the streets finally empty of the hated ocher uniforms of Japan.

The number of people killed during the Rape of Nanking remains under dispute to this day. Japanese nationalist revisionists, flying in the face of overwhelming evidence – including Japanese photographs and the testimony and memoirs of numerous IJA personnel – attempt to declare the number as low as 40,000, or even 10,000.

Though the Japanese destroyed many of their military documents relating to Nanking, and others remain classified by the Japanese government, detailed burial records and Japanese corpse disposal records indicate a minimum of 219,000 victims, of whom 76% consisted of men, 22% of women, and 2% of children of both sexes. Such estimates provide a conservative baseline, considering that the Japanese dumped thousands of bodies in the Yangtze to be carried away and thoroughly cremated thousands of others.

An overall estimate of 250,000 dead appears reasonable, with up to 300,000 possible. Both the United States and the Chinese held war crimes trials for some of the leading perpetrators, though most ordinary soldiers who killed, tortured, and raped men, women, and children escaped any kind of justice and returned quietly to private life.

In sentencing, the International Military Tribunal for the Far East cited a statement issued by Matsui Iwane on October 8th, 1937, containing the typical swaggering braggadocio of IJA pronouncements and indicating his complicity in all of the ensuing slaughters visited on the Chinese:

"The devil-defying sharp bayonets were just on the point of being unsheathed so as to develop their divine influence, and that the mission of the Army was to fulfill all its duties of protecting Japanese residents and interests, and to chastise the Nanking government and the outrageous Chinese." (Brook, 1999, 257).

Matsui Iwane proved slippery and evasive in the witness stand, changing his story repeatedly, sometimes fully acknowledging the horrors committed and revealing some unknown to the Tribunal until that time, at others denying that the Japanese killed or raped anyone in Nanking. He also alternately accepted responsibility and claimed total ignorance of events. His only firm stance centered on deflecting all blame from the Imperial family, even though much evidence pointed to the culpability of Prince Asaka Yasuhiko, who also proved instrumental in the IJA's abandonment of international law.

General Douglas MacArthur, who paradoxically shielded Japanese war criminals, and in particular protected the Japanese imperial family from their obvious guilt in many of Japan's most heinous war crimes, granted immunity from prosecution to Prince Asaka. Matsui hanged, as did six other men. Eighteen more received lighter sentences. In all, the Allies executed only seven men in retribution for the 219,000 or more slaughtered in Nanking.

**Douglas MacArthur**

The Chinese executed four Imperial Japanese officers in their custody following the Nanjing War Crimes Tribunal organized by Chiang Kai-Shek. Of these, Tani Hisao drew the most opprobrium during his trial. Thousands of spectators arrived to watch the isolated figure in the defendants' dock and to listen to the endless litany of horrors recited by hundreds of survivors and other eyewitnesses. The prosecution even brought several mounds of bullet-punctured, blood-stained skulls into the courtroom, excavated from mass graves found beside Nanking's walls.

The court naturally found Tani Hisao guilty and, on April 26th, 1947, Chinese soldiers drove the pinioned general through the streets of Nanking along a route flanked by immense crowds, with a soldier named Tang Zeqi at the wheel. After his parade through the streets, his orders had helped fill with human blood and anguish, the Chinese led Tani to Rain Flower Terrace south of the city. The crowds roared "Revenge!" over and over as the defeated general passed among them.

Finally, at the terrace, a soldier who survived one of the Japanese massacres at Nanking approached Tani from behind and fired a pistol into his head at point blank range. The Chinese judges felt it appropriate that a man nearly killed by Tani's orders should perform the actual execution. A surviving photograph shows the moment of Tani Hisao's death, with the Japanese war criminal jerking forward, and the taller Chinese soldier firing a Hanyang C.96 7.62 mm pistol, copied from the Mauser C96, into his skull. A large crowd of Chinese spectators stands in the background.

As a somber footnote to the colossal Japanese war crime, the pioneering author of the first major book to bring the incident to western attention, Iris Shun-Ru Chang, committed suicide with a revolver near Los Gatos, California on November 9th, 2004. Deeply depressed and haunted by the horrors she researched, and subject to a bout of brief reactive psychosis, along with symptoms of PTSD, Ms. Chang tragically became the final victim of the Nanking Massacre, 67 years after the last shot was fired and the last samurai sword swung in the blood-stained ruins of the martyred city.

**Online Resources**

Other World War II titles by Charles River Editors

Other titles about the rape of Nanking on Amazon

**Bibliography**

Bix, Herbert P. Hirohito and the Making of Modern Japan. New York, 2000.

Brook, Timothy. Documents on the Rape of Nanking. Ann Arbor, 1999.

Chang, Iris. The Rape of Nanking: The Forgotten Holocaust of World War II. New York, 1997.

Hawley, Samuel. The Imjin War: Japan's Sixteenth Century Invasion of Korea and Attempt to Conquer China. London, 2005.

Honda Katsuichi. The Nanjing Massacre: A Japanese Journalist Confronts Japan's National Shame. New York, 2015.

Hu, Hua-ling, and Lian-Hong Zhang. The Undaunted Women of Nanking: The Wartime Diaries of Minnie Vautrin and Tsen Shui-Fang. Carbondale, 2010.

Kaiyuan, Zhang. Eyewitness to Massacre. Armonk, 2001.

Paine, S.C.M. The Wars for Asia, 1911-1949. New York, 2012.

Rabe, John. The Good Man of Nanking: The Diaries of John Rabe. New York, 1998.

Taylor, Jay. The Generalissimo: Chiang Kai-Shek and the Struggle for Modern China. Cambridge,    2009.

Turnbull, Stephen. Samurai Invasion: Japan's Korean War, 1592-1598. London, 2002.

Printed in Great Britain
by Amazon

48953688R00030